W9-BQT-671

Kobe Bryant

Champion Basketball Star

LAKERS

24

SPALDING

Stew Thornley

E **Enslow Publishers, Inc.**
40 Industrial Road
Box 398
Berkeley Heights, NJ 07922
USA

http://www.enslow.com

Original edition published as *Super Sports Star Kobe Bryant* in 2001.

Library of Congress Cataloging-in-Publication Data

Thornley, Stew.
  Kobe Bryant : champion basketball star / Stew Thornley.
    p. cm. — (Sports star champions)
  Includes index.
  Summary: "Explores the life of Kobe Bryant, including his childhood, early basketball career, his many individual
accomplishments, and his NBA championships with the Los Angeles Lakers"—Provided by publisher.
  ISBN 978-0-7660-4029-8
  1. Bryant, Kobe, 1978—Juvenile literature. 2. Basketball players—United States—Biography—Juvenile literature.
I. Title.
  GV884.B794T48 2013
  796.323092—dc23
  [B]
                                        2011038174

Future editions:
Paperback ISBN 978-1-4644-0161-9
ePUB ISBN 978-1-4645-1068-7
PDF ISBN 978-1-4646-1068-4

Printed in the United States of America

052013 Lake Book Manufacturing, Inc., Melrose Park, IL

10 9 8 7 6 5 4 3 2

To Our Readers: We have done our best to make sure all Internet addresses in this book were active and appropriate
when we went to press. However, the author and the publisher have no control over and assume no liability for the material
available on those Internet sites or on other Web sites they may link to. Any comments or suggestions can be sent by e-mail
to comments@enslow.com or to the address on the back cover.

♻ Enslow Publishers, Inc., is committed to printing our books on recycled paper. The paper in every book contains 10% to
30% post-consumer waste (PCW). The cover board on the outside of each book contains 100% PCW. Our goal is to do our
part to help young people and the environment too!

Illustration Credits: AP Images / Branimir Kvartuc, p. 13; AP Images / Chris Pizzello, pp. 6, 26; AP Images / Dusan
Vranic, p. 37; AP Images / Frank Franklin II, p. 43; AP Images / Jim Mone, p. 16; AP Images / Kevork Djansezian, pp. 25,
28, 34; AP Images / Mark J. Terrill, pp. 8, 10, 14, 39, 41; AP Images / Matt A. Brown, p. 33; AP Images / Matt York, p. 18;
AP Images / Michael Conroy, p. 31; AP Images / Rusty Kennedy, pp. 21, 22; AP Images / Tony Gutierrez, pp. 1, 4, 5.

Cover Illustration: AP Images / Tony Gutierrez (Kobe Bryant).

Contents

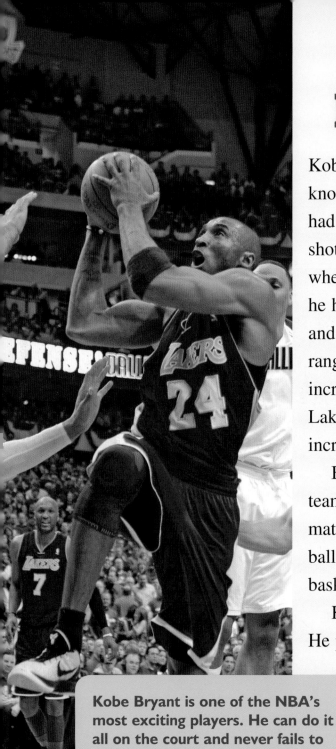

Kobe Bryant is one of the NBA's most exciting players. He can do it all on the court and never fails to give the fans a great performance.

Introduction

Kobe Bryant can do it all. He is best known for scoring points. Once, he had 81 in a single game. Bryant makes shots from all over the court. He shoots when he's off balance. He shoots when he has a defender in his face. He leaps and dunks. He connects from long range. Some of the shots he makes are incredible. Lamar Odom, one of his Lakers teammates, said, "He makes the incredible normal."

Bryant can also pass. When other teams focus on him, it means a teammate is open. Bryant will give up the ball so another player can make an easy basket.

Kobe Bryant is also a great defender. He plays "on-the-belt-buckle defense." That means he guards an opponent so closely that it's like he's attached to his waist. Joe Johnson, a great player for the

Atlanta Hawks, knows what it's like to try and score on Bryant. It's not easy. "Guarding the other team's best player, he'll take that challenge," said Johnson.

Most of all, Bryant helps his team win. The Los Angeles Lakers have won five National Basketball Association (NBA) championships with Bryant. The first three were in the early 2000s. At that time, the Lakers had another great player, Shaquille O'Neal. Recently, Bryant led the Lakers to back-to-back titles with different teammates, such as Odom and Pau Gasol.

Bryant works hard on his game. One summer, he made 100,000 shots. He didn't take 100,000 shots. He made 100,000 shots. Bryant says he doesn't practice taking shots. He practices making them.

Bryant makes shots, he passes, he stops the other team's scorer. He is one of the most exciting players ever.

Most of all, Kobe Bryant is a winner.

Kobe Bryant's work ethic and commitment to practicing his jump shot have made him an all-time great scorer.

Kobe Bryant fights for a loose ball with Celtics forward Rasheed Wallace during Game 7 of the NBA Finals. Although Bryant did not play his best during the game, he never stopped hustling for his team.

A Ring
for Each Finger

Kobe Bryant was tired. He was also struggling. But it may have been the biggest game of his life. He was still determined.

The Los Angeles Lakers were playing the Boston Celtics in the seventh game of the NBA Finals in 2010. Each team had already won three games in the series. The winner of this game would be the champion.

By this time, Bryant owned four championship rings. He received one each time the Lakers won the NBA title since he had joined them in 1996. He wanted another, and he really wanted it this time. The Celtics and Lakers had been

Kobe Bryant grabs a rebound in front of Celtics forward Kevin Garnett. Bryant grabbed 15 rebounds in the decisive game and led the Lakers' comeback in the second half.

rivals for more than fifty years. They had played many great series in the past. Bryant wanted to beat the Celtics.

However, the Celtics were in control. Normally a great shooter, Bryant wasn't on target that night. Boston went ahead by thirteen points early in the second half. "I wanted it so, so bad," Bryant said later. "On top of that, I was on E." (He meant he was running on empty.) "Man, I was really, really tired, and the more I tried to push, the more it kept getting away from me."

Bryant was still confident. He was determined to lead the Lakers back. Bryant kept shooting. He also passed. He played great defense, guarding Boston star point guard Rajon Rondo. He rebounded well.

Bryant and Pau Gasol were dominating on the boards for Los Angeles. They had 33 rebounds between them. That gave the Lakers extra chances at making baskets and kept the Celtics from getting those chances.

The Lakers came back and took the lead. Bryant had the ball. He dribbled in toward Ray Allen, another All-Star for the Celtics. Then he held up and hit a fadeaway jump shot from the right side. It was good, and Los Angeles was up by four points. Later, Bryant had the ball with Allen guarding him again. Bryant went into the air. Instead of shooting, he passed to Ron Artest. Artest buried a three-pointer to make it 79–73 for the Lakers.

Boston came back and closed the gap. Bryant fired a shot. It was no good, but Gasol got the rebound. He passed to Bryant driving in to the basket. Bryant was fouled. He went to the foul line and made both free throws.

With little time left, Boston missed a shot. Gasol grabbed the ball and fired it toward the other end of the court. Bryant raced down to get the ball and dribbled out the final seconds,

Kobe Bryant (center) celebrates with his teammates after winning the 2010 NBA championship. Bryant also won the NBA Finals Most Valuable Player award.

then leaped into the arms of his teammates. The Lakers had won, 83–79. They had beaten the Celtics!

Bryant was named the Most Valuable Player (MVP) of the NBA Finals. It was a great honor, but Bryant was more excited about the Lakers winning. He had his fifth ring and said, "This is the sweetest."

Learning the Game

Kobe Bryant was born on August 23, 1978, in Philadelphia, Pennsylvania. He quickly became a basketball fan. Kobe's dad, Joe Bryant, had played in the NBA. He was a forward for the Philadelphia 76ers in the 1970s. He later played for the San Diego Clippers and the Houston Rockets, before leaving the NBA in 1983. Joe Bryant's nickname was "Jelly Bean," like the candy.

Pam Bryant, Kobe's mom, set up a small basketball court behind their home. That way, Kobe could copy what his dad did. When he was three years old, Kobe began dreaming of someday playing in the NBA.

When Joe Bryant stopped playing in the NBA in 1983, he then played in a professional league in Italy. He brought his family with him. It was a great time for Kobe. He visited many different countries in Europe, and he also learned a new language—Italian.

"It was difficult at first because I couldn't speak Italian," Kobe said. Each day after school, Kobe and his sisters, Shaya and Sharia, got together. They taught each other the new words they had learned that day. "I was able to speak Italian pretty well within a few months," Kobe said.

As he got older, Kobe learned more about basketball. He learned the basic skills first. "I think most kids who grow up

UP CLOSE!

Joe and Pam Bryant also have two daughters, Sharia and Shaya. Kobe was the youngest. Joe and Pam Bryant had gone out to a Japanese restaurant before the birth of their son. They saw "Kobe steak" on the menu. They liked the name, so when their son was born, they named him Kobe.

Kobe Bryant shares a laugh with his father, Joe "Jelly Bean" Bryant, before playing a pickup game in Westchester, California. Kobe got his love of basketball from his father, who he watched play professionally in the **NBA** and in Europe.

Growing up in Italy, Kobe Bryant learned the basic skills of basketball first before trying any fancy moves. This helped him become a good player at a young age. In this photo, Kobe Bryant dribbles around his defender during a playoff game on April 20, 2011.

in America learn all the fancy dribbling," Kobe said later. "In Italy, they teach you the true [basics] and leave out all the nonsense."

Of course, Kobe did learn some fancy moves. But he learned the basics first. That process helped him to become a good player. Playing against his dad also helped Kobe to improve. Every summer, the Bryants came back to Philadelphia where Kobe played in the Sonny Hill League. He struggled at first, but he worked hard and got better.

Jelly Bean Bryant played for eight years in Italy. Then the Bryants moved back to the United States for good in 1991. Kobe was a good player by that time. People were noticing him on the basketball court.

One of the people who noticed Kobe Bryant was Gregg Downer. He was the head basketball coach at Lower Merion High School. Coach Downer knew Kobe was going to be a great player.

When Kobe Bryant was fourteen years old, he tried dunking for the first time. He loved doing it and began practicing the high-flying skill. Soon, Kobe was dunking with ease.

A Basketball Ace

When Kobe Bryant was fourteen years old, he tried something new. He tried dunking the basketball, but it did not turn out very well. "I could barely touch the rim," Kobe said. "It really wasn't a dunk. It was one of those things where you grab the rim and the ball happens to go in. But after that I was really excited. I was really hyped up and dunking was something I worked on."

A lot of things that Kobe tried were difficult at first, but he did not quit. He kept practicing until he was able to do those things at a high level. Kobe also grew a lot in high school. He grew to be six feet six inches tall. With his great

Kobe Bryant played point guard for the Lower Merion High School basketball team. He directed the team's offense on the court and called the plays. Kobe's excellent passing skills made him a great point guard. He still makes great passes playing for the Los Angeles Lakers.

leaping ability, Kobe was soon able to dunk. He could also pass, shoot, dribble, and rebound well.

Kobe became a star on the Lower Merion High School basketball team. In his third year in high school, Kobe scored an average of 31.1 points per game. He also averaged 10.4 rebounds and 5.2 assists. The Lower Merion Aces made it to the state tournament with Kobe leading the team.

Kobe's position on the court was point guard. That is the player who directs the team's offense. He calls the plays. A point guard also has to be able to shoot from the outside, a long distance away from the basket. More important, he has to dribble and pass the ball well. Kobe did all of these things at a high level.

He played against good players during the school year. But he played against even better competition during the summer. Kobe hung out at the gym at St. Joseph's University in Philadelphia. This is where a lot of the players from the Philadelphia 76ers worked out in the summer. Other NBA players who lived in the area also came to that gym.

The players let Kobe join them. Rick Mahorn was one of the NBA players who worked out at St. Joseph's. "He blended in with the rest of us," Mahorn said of Bryant.

"If you can blend with us as a high school player, that says something right there. It says you belong."

Kobe even tried to dunk the ball on Mahorn once. He did not make it, however, Mahorn said, "That's not the point. He actually tried."

Kobe said, "I felt real comfortable all summer with the guys. I had no butterflies, no nothing. [I] never felt intimidated. I could get to the hole [basket]. I could hit the jumper. After a while it kind of popped into my mind that I can play with these guys."

When he started his final year of high school in 1995, Kobe was the best high school player in the country. The Lower Merion Aces were not expected to be as good that year as they had been the year before, however. Some of the better players had graduated, but the team still had Bryant. Early in the season, Lower Merion played Philadelphia Roman Catholic, a team with some talented players. Early in the game, Kobe passed the ball a lot. He set up teammates for easy shots. In the second half, though, Kobe started shooting. He scored on eight straight trips to the basket. Roman Catholic tried double-teaming Bryant, assigning two players to defend him. They even triple-teamed him, with three players defending him. But Bryant kept scoring.

Kobe Bryant dunks the ball during a practice at his Lower Merion High School gym on January 19, 1996. In his senior season, Kobe was considered the best high school player in the country.

Bryant averaged 31 points per game again during his final year at school. And the Lower Merion Aces won the state championship that year.

Bryant also entered the Southeastern Pennsylvania record books for most points scored in a high school career. Kobe had surpassed Wilt Chamberlain's previous record. Chamberlain had played at Overbrook High School in Philadelphia in the 1950s. He later went on to become an all-time great center in the NBA.

Kobe Bryant stands at a podium to announce his decision to skip college and enter the NBA draft at his Lower Merion High School gym on April 29, 1996.

A lot of great players go to college after high school. Kobe could have been a star on any college team in the country. He could also have done well with his studies, too. He was a good student at Lower Merion High School. But he had always wanted to play in the NBA, and he did not want to wait.

In May 1996, he spoke to the students at Lower Merion High School. "I have decided to skip college and take my talents to the NBA. I know I'll have to work extra hard, and I know this is a big step, but I can do it. It's the [chance] of a lifetime. It's time to seize it while I'm young. . . ."

Few players had gone directly from high school into the NBA before Kobe did. Kevin Garnett had done it the year before Bryant. And Garnett did well in his first season with the Minnesota Timberwolves. But many people wondered if Kobe Bryant would do as well. Some people thought Bryant was making a mistake.

Bryant replied, "I've heard a lot of people say I don't have the maturity yet for the NBA. Well, I've seen things in my lifetime that ordinary kids my age haven't seen or experienced. I've been all through Europe, to France, Germany, lived in Italy, been around professional basketball players my whole life. Growing up the way I have, I think I've matured faster than the ordinary person my age."

Tom McGovern was one of the people who agreed with Bryant's decision. McGovern was the athletic director at Lower Merion High School. He said of Bryant, "In the last four years he's brought us joy, happiness, national recognition—and a state title. We will be behind him 100 percent. We owe him that much."

Breaking In

The Charlotte Hornets picked Kobe Bryant in
the first round of the 1996 NBA draft. The draft is how NBA
teams choose new players each year. Bryant never played
for Charlotte, though. Two weeks after the draft took place,
the Hornets traded the young rookie to the Los Angeles
Lakers.

Bryant played in his first game as a member of a NBA
team in early November 1996. He was barely two months
past his eighteenth birthday. The Lakers knew Bryant had a
lot to learn. They did not expect him to be great right away.
Bryant spent a lot of time sitting on the sideline, watching
and learning. But he also got his chances on the court.

Kobe Bryant dunks the ball against the Phoenix Suns on April 11, 1997, during his rookie season. Bryant played his first NBA game just two months after his eighteenth birthday.

Kobe Bryant showed during his rookie season that he could play with the best, but he still had a lot to learn.

He had been a point guard in high school, and he also played that position with the Lakers at times. But he could play at the other guard spot, too, known as the shooting guard. Or he could play at the small forward position, if he was needed there.

Bryant got a chance to play a lot in a game in early January 1997. The Lakers superstar center Shaquille O'Neal had hurt his ankle and could not play. Before the game he told Bryant, "you know what you can do. Go do it, and do it under control."

Bryant played well in that game. He had one dunk that he made after turning completely around on his way up to the basket. He made an even better shot late in the game. The Lakers' lead over the Sacramento Kings was only four points. Los Angeles had the ball, but the shot clock was running out. In the NBA, the shot clock allows only 24 seconds for a player to shoot the ball at the basket. Nick Van Exel of the Lakers threw up a shot. It was off the mark. Bryant swooped in. He grabbed the ball in the air with his back to the basket. He used both hands to tap it in.

A few weeks later, Bryant was put in the starting lineup of his first professional game. Thrilled by the opportunity, Bryant played well, scoring 12 points in a 102–83 win over

Kobe Bryant defends Michael Jordan during a game in Los Angeles on February 1, 1998. Jordan had been one of Bryant's heroes as a kid, and now Bryant had the opportunity to play against him.

the Dallas Mavericks. He played good defense, too. He guarded Jim Jackson and held the Mavericks' star player to only 10 points.

In February, Bryant played against Michael Jordan in a game between the Lakers and the Chicago Bulls. The Lakers beat Chicago by sixteen points. One of the exciting moments came when Bryant blocked one of Jordan's shots.

After the game, Bryant said, "I was about 6 when Jordan came into the league. But I won't back down. My attitude is, you can play basketball, but I can play a little, too."

Ups and Downs

As Kobe Bryant improved and started playing more, the Lakers became the best team in the world. Bryant was matching teammate Shaquille O'Neal as one of the top players in the game.

In 2000, the Lakers made it to the NBA Finals. They beat the Indiana Pacers to win the championship. Not only did Bryant average more than 22 points per game during the regular season, but he was also named to the NBA All-Defensive Team in 1999–2000. He showed people he could play with or without the ball.

Kobe Bryant hoists the NBA championship trophy and Shaquille O'Neal holds the NBA Finals MVP award after the Lakers won the 2002 NBA title. Bryant and O'Neal led the Lakers to three consecutive championships. Unfortunately, the two superstars did not always get along, and O'Neal was traded after the 2004 season.

Bryant and the Lakers weren't done after beating the Pacers. They defeated the Philadelphia 76ers in the finals in 2001 for their second straight title. Bryant was named to the All-NBA team.

In 2002, the Lakers made it three championships in a row, which is called a "three-peat." During the season, Bryant averaged 25 points per game. He was again named to the All-Defensive team. Could it get any better for Bryant and his team?

Before it did, things got worse.

Kobe Bryant had some personal problems in 2003. The Lakers made it to the NBA Finals again in 2004, but this time they were beaten. It also looked like Los Angeles wasn't big enough for both Bryant and Shaquille O'Neal. Sometimes stars clash as they compete for the spotlight, and many fans thought this was the case with Bryant and O'Neal.

O'Neal was traded after the season. Bryant was now the lone star in Los Angeles. He did well, but the Lakers struggled to get back to the top. In 2005–2006, Kobe led the league in scoring, averaging more than 35 points per game. Six times during the year he scored 50 or more points. In one game, he had 62. But his biggest night came in January 2006 when he scored 81 points in a game against the Toronto Raptors. It was the second-highest total ever in a game. Only Wilt Chamberlain, who once had 100 points, had ever scored more than 80 before.

In 2006–2007, Bryant had some incredible games. He scored more than 50 points three times within a month early in the season. Later, he helped the Lakers break a six-game losing streak by scoring 65 points against the Portland Trailblazers. Two nights later, he connected for 50. He got 60 in the next game and, one night later, he had 50 again.

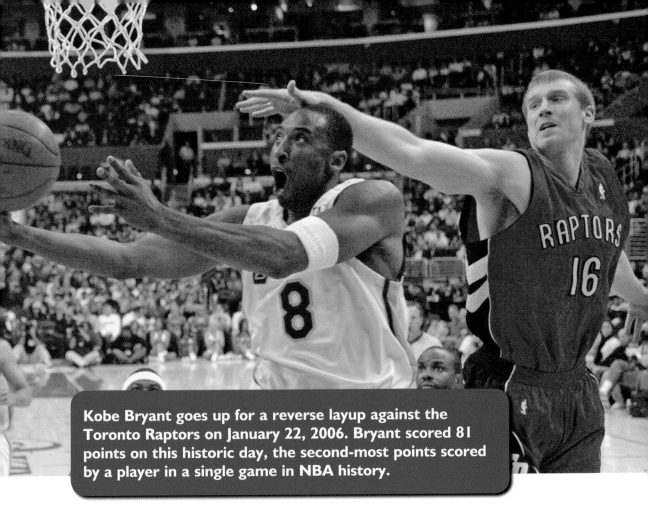

Kobe Bryant goes up for a reverse layup against the Toronto Raptors on January 22, 2006. Bryant scored 81 points on this historic day, the second-most points scored by a player in a single game in **NBA** history.

Bryant had scored 50 points or more in four straight games. For the season, he average more than 30 a game and led the NBA in scoring for the second straight year.

The Lakers were knocked out in the playoffs, though. Finally, in 2008, they made it back to the NBA Finals. The opponent was the Boston Celtics. The Lakers and Celtics have a fierce rivalry. They have often played for the title. It's always a big event when these teams meet.

Kobe Bryant throws down a two-handed dunk during Game 5 of the 2008 NBA Finals. Despite a great effort from the superstar, the Lakers lost to the Celtics in the championship round.

Boston won three of the first five games. One more win for the Celtics would finish the series. The sixth game of the series was played in Boston. It was a bad night for the Lakers. They lost, 131–92.

Boston fans celebrated their championship, but they did more than that. As the Lakers bus left the arena, fans slapped the side of the bus. Some even threw rocks and bottles at it. It was humiliating for the Lakers.

A security guard who was on the bus said, "It was the kind of thing that nobody forgets."

Kobe Bryant definitely would not forget it.

UP CLOSE!

Kobe Bryant has great talent, but he works as hard as anyone to get the most out of it. In the summer of 2003, he worked on his three-point shooting. He would leave the practice court only after making 1,000 shots from beyond the three-point line. The work paid off. Bryant was a great scorer, and, after that, he only got better.

CHAPTER SIX

Back on Top

Before the Lakers started again in 2008, Kobe Bryant had another great opportunity. He was on the United States basketball team in the Olympics. The United States finished first in the Olympic Games in Beijing, China. Kobe had a gold medal, but he had a bigger goal. He wanted to lead his team to another NBA championship.

The Lakers won 65 games with only 17 losses in the 2008–2009 season. They were strong in the playoffs and advanced to the NBA Finals. Their opponents were the Orlando Magic, a good team led by Dwight Howard. Bryant scored 40 points and led Los Angeles to an easy victory in

Kobe Bryant helped lead Team USA to a gold medal in the 2008 Olympic Games in Beijing, China.

the first game. The Lakers went on to win the series, four games to one. Bryant got another championship ring, and he was named MVP of the NBA Finals. He averaged more than 32 points per game against the Magic. He also had more than 7 assists per game.

During the 2009–2010 season, Bryant scored the 25,000th point of his career. This is a huge milestone in basketball. Not only did Bryant reach it, but he also became the youngest player in NBA history to score that many points.

Bryant was still young. However, because he had started playing professionally straight out of high school, he had played a lot of games. The NBA seasons are long, and all the running and physical play causes wear and tear on players. All the games were catching up with Bryant. He struggled with injuries during the season. He even broke the index finger on his shooting hand. But he kept playing.

With a pad on his injured finger, Bryant rolled the ball off his next two fingers when he shot. He even found that this helped his shooting. It created more backspin on the ball. Shots that before would have rolled off the rim were going in now. Four nights after he broke his finger, Bryant scored 42 points against the Chicago Bulls. The next night,

Kobe Bryant goes up for a jump shot during Game 2 of the 2009 NBA Finals against the Orlando Magic.

he scored 39 points against the Milwaukee Bucks, which included a game-winning basket in overtime.

Bryant was struggling with other aches and pains, and they affected his shooting. Some people said he should take a break to let the injuries heal. But Bryant carried on. "If I can help the team win, I'll play, even if I'm not putting up great numbers."

He finally missed some games in February after he sprained his ankle. The Lakers were on their way, though. With Bryant back, Los Angeles made it to the NBA Finals for the third year in a row.

The opponent was the Boston Celtics. It was payback time.

The teams split the first four games. The Celtics won the next one and were only a win away from taking the title. The series came back to Los Angeles. The Lakers needed to win twice to avoid defeat.

Facing elimination, Los Angeles won Game 6 by twenty-two points. The entire season would come down to one game. It was a close one. The Celtics opened up a thirteen-point lead in the second half. But the Lakers battled back.

In the final game, Bryant led all scorers with 23 points. The Lakers won, 83–79, for their second title in a row. They had beaten the hated Celtics.

Kobe Bryant takes an off-balance jump shot over Boston Celtics guard Rajon Rondo during Game 6 of the 2010 NBA Finals. The Lakers won the hard-fought series in Game 7.

Bryant had another good year in 2010–2011. He averaged more than 24 points per game for the eleventh year in a row. The Lakers finished first in their division again. However, they were knocked out of the playoffs in the second round by the Dallas Mavericks. Bryant would be back for more, and he would help the Lakers try again.

Bryant is great on the court. He also enjoys his time off it. He and his wife, Vanessa, have two daughters, Natalia and Gianna. Bryant has other talents besides basketball, such as poetry. "Writing poetry is a great way to express myself," he said.

But it's his skills in the arena that make him stand out. In the 1990s, Bryant was a rising star who looked up to the great players in the game. Now rising stars are looking up to him. One is Kevin Durant of the Oklahoma City Thunder. "He has those championship rings," said Durant. "It's a level I'm trying to reach."

Bryant uses his fame to help people. He has a foundation that provides young people with scholarships, leadership grants, and cultural exchanges. He has also granted more wishes than any NBA player through the Make-a-Wish Foundation.

Kobe Bryant takes a jump shot against the New York Knicks on February 11, 2011. Bryant averaged more than 24 points per game for the eleventh season in a row.

When Bryant started with the Lakers, he wore the number 8 on his jersey. Now he wears number 24. He uses this number on his Web site, which allows fans to follow Bryant's playing career and find out a lot of other information about the superstar.

Kobe Bryant still has more basketball to play. He wants to win more NBA championships in Los Angeles. Although his career isn't over, Bryant has already cemented his legacy as one of the NBA's greatest players of all time.

UP CLOSE!

Grauman's Chinese Theater in Hollywood honors people in a special way. They are allowed to put their hand and footprints, along with their autograph, in wet cement. Most who get to do this are actors and actresses. In 2011, Kobe Bryant became the first athlete to be honored in this way.

Career Statistics

NBA REGULAR-SEASON STATISTICS WITH THE LOS ANGELES LAKERS												
Year	GP	Min.	FGM	FGA	FG%	FT%	Reb.	Ast.	Stl.	Blk.	Pts.	PPG
1996–1997	71	1,103	176	422	.417	.889	132	91	49	23	539	7.6
1997–1998	79	2,056	391	913	.428	.794	242	199	74	40	1,220	15.4
1998–1999	50	1,896	362	779	.465	.839	264	190	72	50	996	19.9
1999–2000	66	2,524	554	1,183	.468	.821	416	323	106	62	1,485	22.5
2000–2001	68	2,783	701	1,510	.464	.853	399	338	114	43	1,938	28.5
2001–2002	80	3,063	749	1,597	.469	.829	441	438	118	35	2,019	25.2
2002–2003	82	3,401	868	1,924	.451	.843	564	481	181	67	2,461	30.0
2003–2004	65	2,447	516	1,178	.438	.852	359	330	112	28	1,557	24.0
2004–2005	66	2,689	573	1,324	.433	.816	392	398	86	53	1,819	27.6
2005–2006	80	3,277	978	2,173	.450	.850	425	360	147	30	2,832	35.4
2006–2007	77	3,140	813	1,757	.463	.868	439	413	111	36	2,430	31.6
2007–2008	82	3,192	775	1,690	.459	.840	517	441	151	40	2,323	28.3
2008–2009	82	2,960	800	1,712	.467	.856	429	399	120	37	2,201	26.8
2009–2010	73	2,835	716	1,569	.456	.811	391	365	113	20	1,970	27.0
2010–2011	82	2,779	740	1,639	.451	.828	419	388	99	12	2,078	25.3
TOTALS	1,103	40,145	9,712	21,370	.454	.837	5,829	5,154	1,653	576	27,868	25.3

GP–Games Played
Min.–Minutes Played
FGM–Field Goals Made

FGA–Field Goals Attempted
FG%–Field Goal Percentage
FT%–Free Throw Percentage

Reb.–Rebounds
Ast.–Assists
Stl.–Steals

Blk.–Blocked Shots
Pts.–Points Scored
PPG–Points per Game

Where to Write to Kobe Bryant

Mr. Kobe Bryant
c/o The Los Angeles Lakers
Staples Center
1111 S. Figueroa St.
Los Angeles, CA 90015

Glossary

assist—A pass to a teammate who makes a basket.

double-teaming—Two defenders guarding one player.

draft—The way NBA teams choose new players each year.

dunk—A shot that is slammed through the basket from directly above the basket. Also known as a slam or slam dunk.

fadeaway—A shot taken while falling away from the basket.

outside shot—A shot taken a long distance away from the basket.

rebound—Getting the basketball after a missed shot.

shot clock—A clock that limits the amount of time to shoot the ball. The shot clock in the NBA is twenty-four seconds.

triple-teaming—Three defenders guarding one player.

Further Reading

Books

Doeden, Matt. *The World's Greatest Basketball Players.* Mankato, Minn.: Capstone Press, 2010.

Frisch, Aaron. *Los Angeles Lakers.* Mankato, Minn.: Creative Education, 2011.

Gitlin, Marty. *Kobe Bryant: NBA Champion.* Edina, Minn.: ABDO Publishing Company, 2011.

Savage, Jeff. *Kobe Bryant.* Minneapolis, Minn.: Lerner Publications Company, 2011.

Woods, Mark. *Basketball Legends.* New York: Crabtree Publishing Company, 2009.

Internet Addresses

KB24.com: Kobe Bryant's Official Web site
<http://www.kb24.com/>

NBA.com: Kobe Bryant Player Profile
<http://www.nba.com/home/playerfile/kobe_bryant/>

The Official Site of the Los Angeles Lakers
<http://www.nba.com/lakers/>

Index

A

Allen, Ray, 9

Artest, Ron, 9

awards, honors

  most points scored, 21, 38, 42

  Most Valuable Player (MVP), 10, 38

B

basketball career

  high school, 17–21

  injuries, 38–40

  inspiration for, 11, 20

  Italy, 12–15

  NBA beginning, 22–24

  practice habits, 5, 17–19, 35

Boston Celtics, 7–10, 33–35, 40

Bryant, Joe "Jelly Bean", 11–15

Bryant, Kobe

  birth, childhood, 11–15

  overview, 4–5, 42–44

  scoring averages, 32–33

  versatility of, 27

Bryant, Pam, 11, 12

Bryant, Sharia, 12

Bryant, Shaya, 12

C

Chamberlain, Wilt, 21, 32

Charlotte Hornets, 24

Chicago Bulls, 29, 38

D

Dallas Mavericks, 29, 42

Downer, Gregg, 15

G

Garnett, Kevin, 23

Gasol, Pau, 5, 9

I

Indiana Pacers, 30

Italy, 12–15

J

Jordan, Michael, 29

L

Los Angeles Lakers

  Bryant in starting lineup, 27–29

  as champions with Bryant, 5

  NBA Finals (2000), 30

  NBA Finals (2001, 2002), 31

  NBA Finals (2008), 33–35

  NBA Finals (2009), 36–38

  NBA Finals (2010), 7–10, 38–40

Lower Merion High School, 15, 17–23

M

Mahorn, Rick, 19–20

McGovern, Tom, 23

Minnesota Timberwolves, 23

O

Olympic Games, 36

O'Neal, Shaquille, 5, 27, 30, 32

P

Philadelphia 76ers, 11, 19, 31

point guard, 19, 27

Portland Trailblazers, 32

R

Rondo, Rajon, 9

S

Sacramento Kings, 27

San Diego Clippers, 11

Sonny Hill League, 15

T

Toronto Raptors, 32